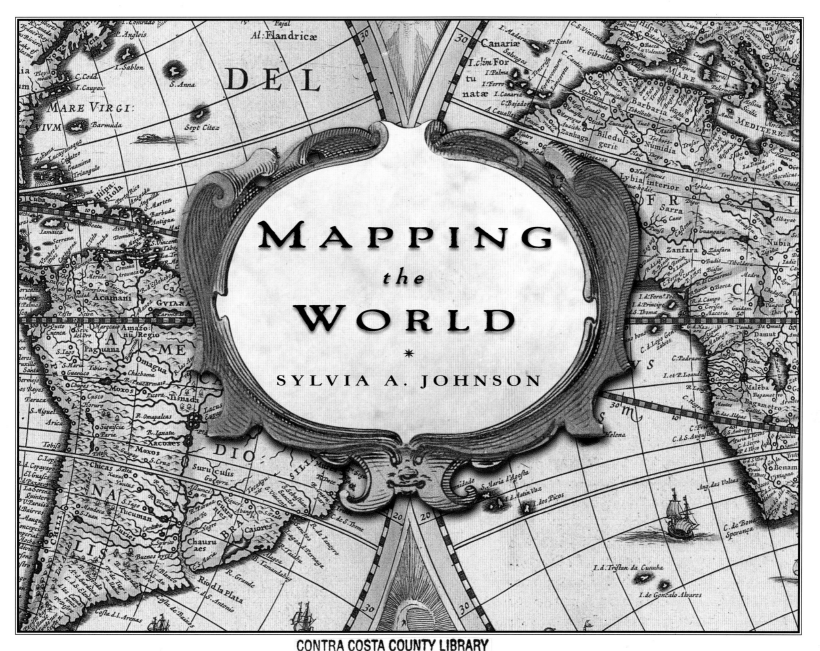

Mapping the World

*

Sylvia A. Johnson

Atheneum Books for Young Readers

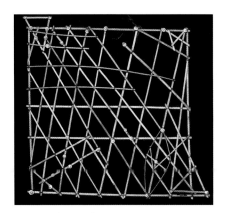

This map was made by the people of the Marshall Islands, who sailed their outrigger canoes
in the waters of the Pacific Ocean. It uses shells to represent islands and strips
of palm fiber to show the direction and pattern of waves.

Atheneum Books for Young Readers
An imprint of Simon & Schuster Children's Publishing Division
1230 Avenue of the Americas
New York, New York 10020

Book design by Michael Nelson
The text of this book is set in Horley Old style

Printed in Hong Kong
10 9 8 7 6 5 4 3 2 1

Library of Congress Cataloging-in-Publication Data
Johnson, Sylvia A.
Mapping the world / by Sylvia A. Johnson.—1st ed.
p. cm.
Includes bibliographical references.
Summary: A history of mapmaking showing how
maps both reflect and change people's view
of the world.

ISBN 0-689-81813-0

1. Cartography—History—Juvenile literature.
2. Geography, Ancient—Maps—Juvenile literature.
[1. Cartography—History. 2. Maps.] I. Title.
GA105.6.J65 1999 912—dc21 98-7858

FIRST
EDITION

CONTENTS

PICTURES OF THE WORLD

In 1962, John Glenn, the first American astronaut to orbit the earth, looked down from his Mercury spacecraft and commented that he could see the features of the planet "laid out just like on a map." Since the 1960s, everyone has seen the spectacular photographs of the earth viewed from space. We know that the boot of Italy, the great bulge of Africa, and the narrow isthmus that connects North and South America do indeed look just as they do on maps in atlases and geography books. But maps have not always presented such an accurate picture of the physical world.

Today's mapmakers, or cartographers, use computers, sophisticated measuring instruments, and other tools of modern science. Mapmakers of the past did not have these resources. They based their images of the world on their own limited observations and on the reports of travelers returning from distant lands. Sometimes their ideas about the physical world were shaped by legends or religious beliefs. Religion, politics, military power—all these things influenced the way that a mapmaker pictured the world.

Whether they are based on the reports of travelers or on the latest images from space, all maps have stories to tell. Who was the mapmaker? How was the map made, and for what purpose? And finally, what kind of world do we see reflected in its lines and shapes?

The map carved on this small clay tablet is one of the oldest pictures of the world known today. Made around 500 B.C. in Babylonia (modern Iraq), it shows the earth as a flat disk surrounded by a ring of ocean. At the top is the curved line of a mountain range, and flowing from it, the broad Euphrates River, which passes through a rectangle representing the capital city, Babylon. Circles near the edge of the disk show the lands of the Assyrians and Chaldeans, Babylonia's neighbors. Beyond the ocean are islands represented by triangles, only one of which has survived intact. These islands were home to creatures described in Babylonian legends.

We know what many of the features in this map represent because they are labeled in cuneiform, the wedge-shaped writing used by the Babylonians. Without these labels, the map would mean little today. The physical world has not changed much since Babylonian times, but the way that people see it has changed tremendously. The maker of this small clay map showed what was important to the people of Babylonia—the distant sea, the life-giving river, the neighboring kingdoms that could threaten their existence. On the edge of the world were lands described in legends. What existed beyond this narrow frame? The mapmaker didn't know, and had no reason to care.

THE FIRST CARTOGRAPHER

Around A.D. 150, an important Greek mapmaker and geographer named Claudius Ptolemaeus, or Ptolemy (TAHL-uh-mee), lived and worked in Alexandria, a city in North Africa that was part of the Roman Empire. The map on page 7 pictures Ptolemy's world, but it was made more than one thousand years after his death. Created in 1482, the map was based on information in a book that Ptolemy had written.

Ptolemy was a scholar who studied astronomy and geography, which he defined as "a representation in pictures of the whole known world together with the parts contained therein." In his book about geography, he included detailed discussions of maps and how they should be made. Like all educated people of his time, Ptolemy knew that the earth was shaped like a sphere. He worked out several ways of picturing the round earth on a flat surface, and this map uses one of them. Drawn to look like a section of a sphere, it is covered by a pattern of curved lines.

The human heads on the borders of Ptolemy's map represent the twelve prevailing winds recognized in ancient times.

In his book, Ptolemy explained how these intersecting lines of latitude and longitude, which were based on astronomical observations, could be used to locate places on a map. He provided the locations of hundreds of cities, rivers, and mountain ranges in southern Europe, northern Africa, even in distant India. Little was known about the lands in the far north and south, but Ptolemy, like most people of his day, believed that these areas were too cold for human life.

Ptolemy's world looks more familiar to us than the world pictured on the Babylonian map, but it has some strange features. For example, it shows the Indian Ocean (lower right) enclosed by a body of land that joins Africa in the west and Asia in the east. Ptolemy just assumed that this land existed because the great continent of Asia in the northern part of the earth had to be balanced by an equally large body of land in the south.

The world's first great cartographer, Ptolemy had an im-

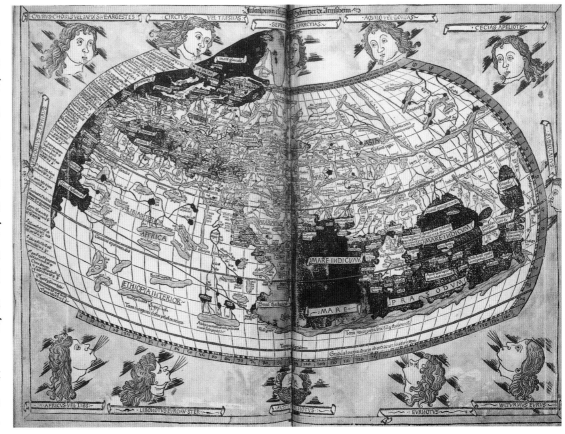

mense influence on later mapmakers, but many years would pass before his ideas became widely known. Beginning around A.D. 400, the Greek and Roman civilization of which Ptolemy had been a part crumbled under the attack of invaders. During the violent period that followed, Ptolemy's book about geography disappeared from western Europe. But in the eastern city of Byzantium and in the lands ruled by Arab powers, knowledge of Ptolemy's work and even copies of his book survived. When this knowledge was brought back to Europe in the 1400s, it would change the way that Europeans saw the world.

A World of Faith

This simple map represents a way of looking at the world that is very different from Ptolemy's view. Originally created around A.D. 600 by a priest and scholar named Isidore of Seville, it was popular in Europe during the Middle Ages. Known as a T-O map because of its basic shape, it shows the world as a disk surrounded by ocean. Within this "O" are three continents separated by three important bodies of water, which make up the "T." The vertical bar of the T represents the Mediterranean Sea, while the crossbar stands for two rivers, the Nile and the Don.

The features of a T-O map reflect the powerful role of Christianity in Europe during the Middle Ages. East is at the top of the map not only because the sun rises in the east, but also because it is the location of the Garden of Eden as described in the Bible. Other references to the Bible are found on the continents of Asia, Africa, and Europe, which are labeled with the names of Noah's three sons. According to the Book of Genesis, the earth was divided among these three after the Flood.

During the Middle Ages, more elaborate circular maps were also used to portray the world as seen through the eyes of Christian faith. Historians often use the Latin name *mappa mundi* ("map of the world") for one of these maps. The beautiful example shown on page 9 was part of a psalter, or book of psalms, made in England around A.D. 1250. The mapmaker is unknown but was probably a monk who spent his life copying books by hand and illustrating them.

In the psalter map, as in the T-O map, east is at the top, marked with the beaming face of the rising sun. Under the sun is the Garden of Eden, indicated by the heads of Adam and Eve enclosed in a circle. To the right of Eden is the Red Sea (colored red as it usually is in maps from this period), while at the very center of the map is the holy city of Jerusalem.

Other features of this *mappa mundi* are not so easy to identify today. For example, what is that rough semicircle shown on the upper left? People of the 1200s would immediately have recognized this as representing a wall made out of iron and brass. According to stories popular in the Middle Ages, the conqueror Alexander the Great had built this high wall somewhere in the north to protect the civilized world from the armies of Gog and Magog, evil forces described in the Bible.

Ptolemy believed that maps should show the exact location of places in the physical world, but the maker of the psalter map did not share this concern. He was more interested in religion than in geography. In his view, the Garden of Eden and the land of Gog and Magog were places just as real and important as Jerusalem or the Red Sea. All were part of the world of Christian belief, symbolized by the majestic figure of Christ that appears at the top of the map. In his left hand, Christ holds a small T-O globe, another image of the world that he ruled.

A MEDIEVAL ROAD MAP

Not all maps from the Middle Ages were expressions of religious belief. Some were concerned with practical matters, such as everyday travel. A good example is this road map made by an English monk named Matthew Paris sometime during the 1200s.

The Romans had made maps of the roads in their vast empire on long narrow pieces of parchment (animal skin) that could be rolled up and carried by travelers. Matthew Paris's road maps are similar to these earlier maps. They are made up of narrow strips that show only roads and important places along them. Notes written on the maps tell the traveler how

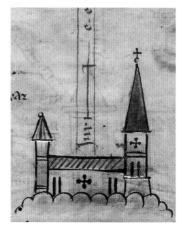

A French church on Matthew Paris's pilgrimage route.

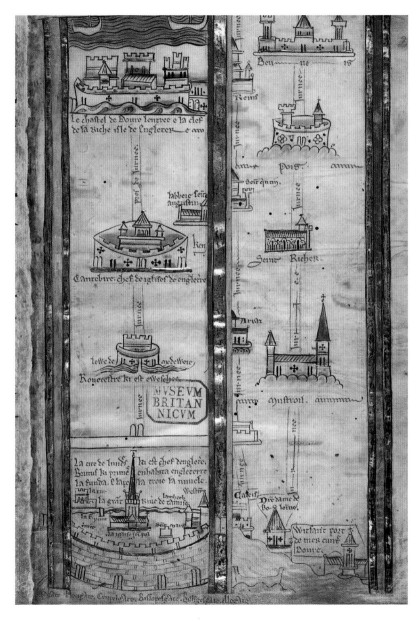

many days it will take to get from one stop to the next.

Paris's road maps were made mainly for the use of pilgrims traveling to Christian shrines and holy places. They were included in pilgrim guidebooks. This is a page from one of these books containing two map strips. The maps show a route that began in London (lower left), then made its way across the English Channel (upper left and lower right), through France, and into Italy. Here pilgrims would board ships that would take them to their final destination, Jerusalem.

To modern eyes, Matthew Paris's maps look a lot like the route maps provided by auto clubs today. They show roads as straight lines, with no indication of any changes in direction. Information important to travelers—where to stop, how long the journey will take—is supplied, but the surrounding country is not shown. Like auto club route maps, Matthew Paris's maps were made strictly for getting from place to place. The mapmaker did not need to present a picture of the whole world.

Here is another guide for travelers—a sea chart used by European sailors of the 1400s. Sea charts, or portolan charts, first appeared in Europe in the early 1300s. Before that time, mariners had depended on written manuals, called *portolani* in Italian, which described landmarks along the coasts where they navigated their ships. Eventually, drawings were added to these mariners' guides, and the *portolani* became portolan charts.

This portolan chart was made in 1489 by Albini de Canepa, a chart maker who lived in the Italian seaport of Genoa. Drawn by hand on a piece of parchment, it presents a detailed picture of coastlines around the Mediterranean and in northern Europe. The names of harbors, bays, and other landmarks are written at right angles to the coasts, with the most important harbors—for example, Jaffa at the eastern end of the Mediterranean—shown in red. To aid sailors in navigation, the chart maker has marked the location of hazards such as rocks and shallow water with crosses or x marks.

The most important part of a portolan chart was the network of fine lines that covered it, radiating out from figures called compass roses. With the help of these lines and a real compass, sailors could navigate not just along the coasts but across open sea. For example, to plot a course from Genoa to Tripoli in North Africa, a ship captain would place a ruler on his chart between the two locations. Then he would find the line that most closely paralleled this route and trace it to the nearest compass rose.

A compass rose represented a compass face and was marked

off in directions—south, south-by-southwest, etc. By noting where his line intersected the compass rose, the captain knew in what direction to steer his ship. Readings from a real compass and other instruments would guide him on the way to his destination.

Since portolan charts were meant for use by mariners, they showed few land features. Like Canepa's chart, however, they often included beautifully colored pictures

that told something about the world. Canepa uses long, bumpy shapes to represent mountain ranges and includes little pictures of important cities such as Jerusalem and Genoa. Tents stand for the realms of Muslim rulers in Africa and nomadic tribes in Asia.

Although portolan charts often included such fascinating details, their main purpose was as a tool of navigation. And they served this purpose well—as long as European sailors stayed close to home. When their ships entered unknown waters, the portolan charts offered little guidance.

A Map of a New World

This timeworn parchment, with its intersecting lines and compass roses, looks a lot like Albini de Canepa's portolan chart. But the world shown here is nothing like the one that Canepa knew. Discovered in a Paris antique shop in 1832, this map was made around 1500 by Juan de la Cosa, a Spanish navigator and shipowner. De la Cosa was not just any ordinary seafarer. He traveled with Christopher Columbus on his second voyage of exploration in 1493, and his map is the first to show the new lands that the explorers found across the Ocean Sea.

Most of Juan de la Cosa's map pictures the familiar old world of Europe, Africa, and Asia, but on one end of the long parchment are shapes that have never appeared before on European maps. Take a close look, and you will see the islands of the Caribbean drawn in some detail. Columbus made his first two landings in these islands, and de la Cosa must have been very familiar with them.

The large dark areas on the end of the parchment represent the continents of North and South America. In 1500, very little was known about these mysterious lands. John Cabot had reached North America in 1497, and Columbus had landed on the coast of South America the following year. De la Cosa's map was probably based on the vague reports of these and other early explorers.

When Juan de la Cosa made his map, did he know that he was picturing not just new territory but a new

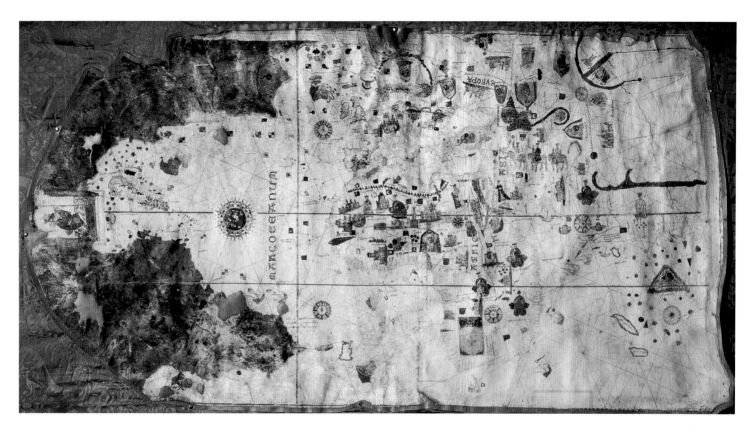

world? Historians are still arguing about the answer to this question. Christopher Columbus insisted that the lands he had found were in Asia. In fact, he made the members of his crew, including de la Cosa, swear they would support his claim that the island of Cuba was part of the mainland of China. But de la Cosa's map shows that Cuba is definitely an island.

Because North and South America are cut off at the end of the map, it is difficult to know how de la Cosa meant to show them. Are those dark shapes supposed to be part of Asia, which appears on the other end of the parchment? Or could they be the edge of a vast new world? The map gives no clue as to what was in the mapmaker's mind.

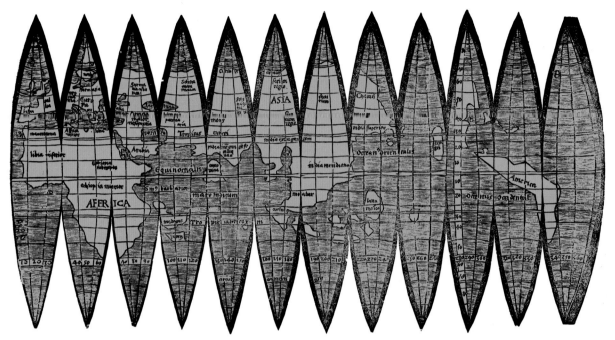

This strangely shaped drawing doesn't look much like the other maps in this book. In fact, it is part of a globe. If it were cut out and glued to a sphere, the individual sections, called gores, would come together to make a complete image of the world.

While not very useful for navigation, globes present an accurate image of the round earth, and European cartographers had made them for centuries. These globe gores were created in 1507 by an influential German mapmaker named Martin Waldseemüller.

Like most educated Europeans of his day, Waldseemüller had heard all about the discoveries of Columbus and other explorers. He was one of the first mapmakers to suggest that the lands they had found were not part of Asia but a whole new world previously unknown to the people of Europe. The New World continents that Waldseemüller pictures on his globe gores (on the far right) don't look like the familiar shapes we know today. But the mapmaker clearly shows that these lands are separated from Asia by a wide stretch of ocean.

Martin Waldseemüller's pictures of the New World had a bigger impact than the mapmaker could ever have imagined. On his globe gores and on a large world map that he also produced in 1507, Waldseemüller put the word *America* on the southern continent. He did this to honor the Italian explorer Amerigo Vespucci, who had made expeditions to the New World soon after Columbus.

Waldseemüller's 1507 maps with the name *America* on them were very popular. More than a thousand copies of the large world map were printed on the recently developed printing press. Waldseemüller also published a book in which he praised Amerigo Vespucci's contributions. Soon people all over Europe were calling the New World lands by the name Waldseemüller had chosen.

The mapmaker was later sorry that he had selected Vespucci rather than Columbus for this honor, but his change of mind came too late. The Americas had been named. Whether the lands already had names given by their original inhabitants, Europeans didn't bother to ask.

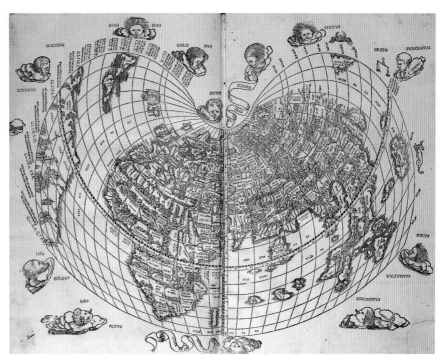

When Ptolemy's book on geography reappeared in Europe in the mid-1400s, mapmakers eagerly studied it and began making maps based on the Greek cartographer's ideas. In this map from 1511, the new lands of the Americas (far left) have been added to Ptolemy's world.

A Land of Cannibals

By the mid-1500s, when this map was created, Europeans knew much more about the New World than in Waldseemüller's day. Explorers such as Balboa and Verrazano had ventured beyond the eastern coasts into the interior of the new lands. In 1519, Ferdinand Magellan, seeking a route to Asia, had sailed from Spain on a voyage that would take him around South America and into the Pacific Ocean. Magellan was killed in the Philippines, but one of his ships made it back to Spain in 1522, completing the first voyage around the world.

This map of the Americas by a prominent German mapmaker, Sebastian Münster, includes information about South America based on Magellan's expedition. Münster shows the straits at the tip of the continent that were named after the great explorer. He even pictures Magellan's ship, the *Victoria,* sailing proudly in the Pacific (and apparently heading in the wrong direction).

Münster's map also includes a scene that illustrated a common European belief about South America—that it was a land of cannibals. The mapmaker pictures the remains of a cannibal feast on the eastern side of the continent.

Sebastian Münster's New World map was included in a book he wrote that was published in 1546. By this time, printing had become common in Europe, and printing presses were turning out hundreds of books, maps, and other documents. Münster's map, like many produced during this period, was made from a woodcut, an image carved on a block of wood that was inked and pressed onto a sheet of paper. Black ink was used for the lines, and colors were then added by hand to individual copies. Even when maps became more elaborate and detailed than Münster's simple woodcut (for example, the Hondius map on page 23), they were almost always hand-painted. It was not until the 1800s that newer printing methods would make it possible to print maps in color.

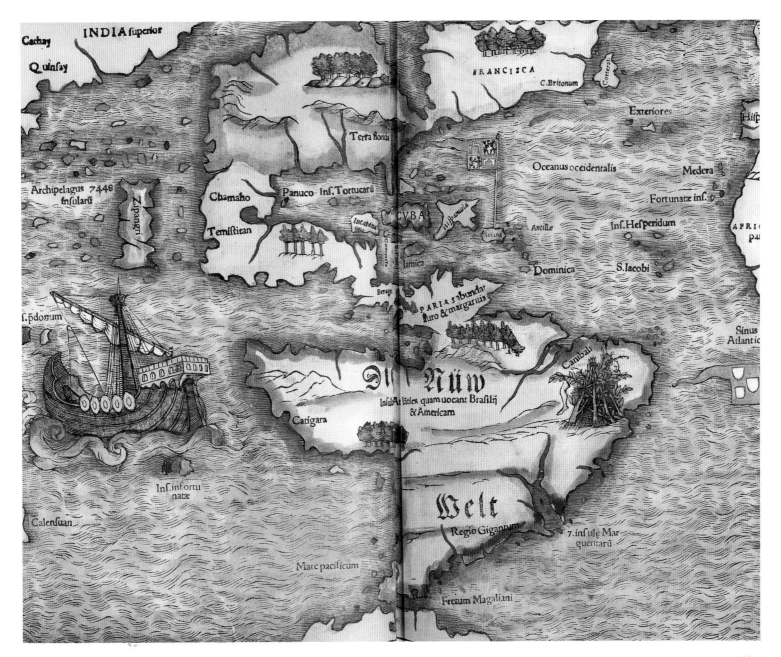

INDIA superior

Cathay

Quinsay

Archipelagus 7448 Insularū

Zipangri

s.f.pdorum

Inf.infortunatæ

Calenſuan

Chamaho

Temistitan

Catigara

Mare pacificum

Panuco· Inf.Tortucarū

Iucatana

Cosmetta

Terra florida

CVBA

Hispaniola

Sciana

Jamica

Beragy

PARIA ſabundat auro & margaritis

Nüw
Insulä lätius quam uocant Brasilij & Americam

Welt
Regio Gigantum

Fretum Magaliani

FRANCISCA

C.Britonum

Cortere

Exteriores

Oceanus occidentalis

Antillæ

Dominica

Canibali

Medera

Fortunatæ inf.

Inf.Hesperidum

S.Iacobi

7.insulę Margueritarū

His

AFRI p

Sinus Atlantic

19

THE FIRST ATLAS

The 1400s and 1500s were exciting times for mapmakers in Europe. Soon after Ptolemy was rediscovered in the mid-1400s, explorers began returning with new information that greatly expanded Ptolemy's image of the world. At first, mapmakers attempted to add this information to Ptolemy's maps. Finally, they decided that it was time to put Ptolemy aside and to take a new look at the world.

In 1570, Abraham Ortelius published a whole book of maps based on the most up-to-date information available. Ortelius was a native of the Netherlands, where the best European mapmakers and printers lived during the 1500s. To produce his book, he collected maps made by cartographers all over Europe. Then he had the maps redrawn in a uniform size and style and printed them using the method of copperplate engraving, which produced a much finer image than woodcuts. Ortelius called his book of maps *Theatrum Orbis Terrarum*, Latin for "Theater of the World." It was the first modern atlas.

The map on page 21, which appeared in the 1571 edition of Ortelius's atlas, shows the world as it was known to the people of the late 1500s. Its oval framework includes the continents of both the Old World and the New. The map also shows Terra Australis (the Southern Land), a part of Ptolemy's world that Europeans refused to give up.

Ptolemy had believed in a large southern continent, and Ortelius, like most mapmakers of the 1500s, always included it in his maps even though Magellan and other explorers had found no evidence of Terra Australis. On this map, he labeled the continent *Terra Australis Nondum Cognita*—"The Southern Land Not Yet Known." In 1605, Dutch explorers discovered a landmass that would be called Australia, but it was nothing like the great southern land dreamed of for centuries. It was not until the late 1800s that Europeans finally reached Antarctica, the ice-covered continent at the bottom of the world.

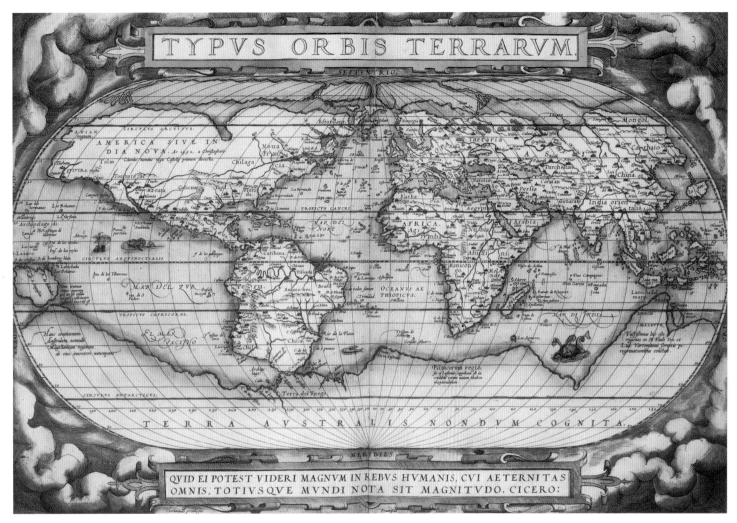

Ortelius's map pictures another dream of European explorers—the Northwest Passage. This channel of open water north of Europe, Asia, and North America was supposed to connect the lands of the Old and New Worlds. For hundreds of years, explorers searched for the Northwest Passage, and many lost their lives in the attempt. The northern water route does exist, but it is clogged with ice most of the year and can be navigated only by ice-breaking ships or submarines.

A World in Two Hemispheres

When Abraham Ortelius published his collection of maps in 1570, another mapmaker in the Netherlands was working on an atlas. Gerardus Mercator was the first to use the word *atlas,* taking the name from the Greek god who supported the universe on his shoulders. Mercator's three-volume atlas, completed after his death in 1594, became famous throughout Europe. Then in the early 1600s, a Dutch engraver named Jodocus Hondius bought the printing plates for Mercator's atlas maps. On this foundation, Hondius and his family built a thriving business as mapmakers.

The world map on the opposite page appeared in an atlas published by Jodocus Hondius's son Henricus in 1633. Like most maps of this period, it presents the world in twin hemispheres that look something like two sides of a globe. The spheres are surrounded by an elaborate border filled with scenes and portraits of important people. In the lower right corner is a picture of Jodocus Hondius, the founder of the mapmaking firm, while on the lower left is his famous predecessor Mercator. Ptolemy (upper right), the cartographer

of the ancient world, is shown dressed in the style of the 1400s, the period in which his influential book was reintroduced in Europe. The fourth figure is Julius Caesar, who was believed to have ordered the mapping of the Roman world.

The world shown in Hondius's map was not quite the same as the world had Ortelius pictured. Terra

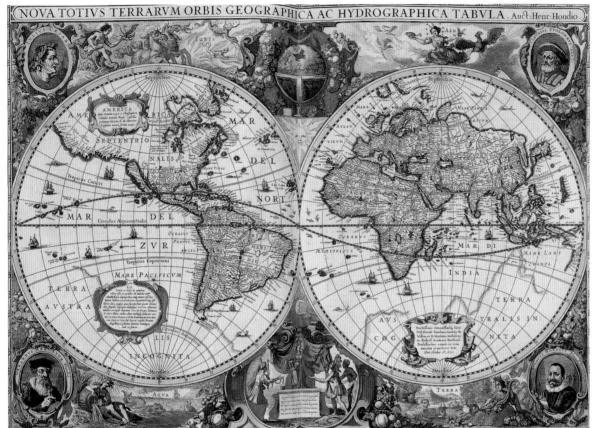

NOVA TOTIVS TERRARVM ORBIS GEOGRAPHICA AC HYDROGRAPHICA TABVLA. Auct: Henr: Hondio.

These figures from the lower map border represent water and earth, two of the four elements of the universe. Fire and air appear at the top of the map.

Australis is still there, but its outline is vague, as if the mapmaker is not so sure about the southern continent.

If you look at North America, you will see another change—a large island has appeared just off the continent's western coast. This is the mapmaker's representation of Baja California. On Ortelius's map, the region is shown correctly as a peninsula, but by Henricus Hondius's time, it had been transformed into an island. Historians believe that a mistake made on a single map published in the early 1600s was picked up by later mapmakers and copied again and again. It was not until the mid-1700s that Baja California was put back where it belonged.

Ever since Ptolemy, mapmakers had been experimenting with different map projections, or methods of picturing the round earth on a flat sheet of paper. By the 1800s, one projection had won out over all the others. The Mercator projection, created by the great cartographer of the 1500s, was used on all kinds of maps.

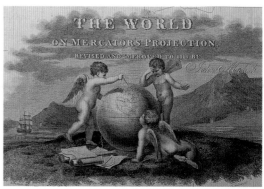

This world map, made in 1818 by the American mapmaker John Melish, uses the Mercator projection. This fact is proudly proclaimed on the cartouche (kar-TOOSH), the decorative label that contains the map's title. Melish was one of the first people in the United States to make a living producing maps. He wanted to provide Americans with the best geographical information, and in the 1800s, that meant using Mercator's projection.

Originally developed for use on sea charts, the Mercator projection was a way to represent the curve of the earth while still showing latitude and longitude as straight lines. If you look at a globe, you will see that the vertical lines of longitude come closer and closer together until they meet at the poles. But how do you show this on a large rectangular map? Before Mercator, most mapmakers used equal spaces between lines of longitude and latitude, creating a neat pattern of squares and right angles. But this system ignored the round shape of the earth and created problems for sailors navigating over long distances.

Gerardus Mercator came up with a clever way to solve all these problems. He left the lines of longitude equally spaced but gradually *increased* the space between the lines of latitude toward the North and South Poles. (You can see this on Melish's map.) This made up for the fact that on a map, lines of longitude in the area of the poles are farther apart than they would be on a sphere. Increasing the space between *latitude* lines balanced out this difference and kept the correct relationship between the two sets of lines.

First introduced in 1569, Mercator's map projection was not immediately popular, but sailors soon discovered its usefulness. From the 1700s on, most sea charts were based on this projection. As a way of presenting an image of the world, however, it had some serious drawbacks. For example, because the projection is stretched toward the poles, it exaggerates the size of landmasses in these regions. On a map using the Merca-

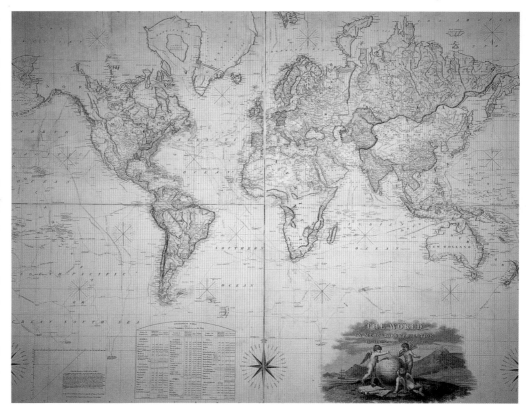

tor projection, the northern island of Greenland appears to be seventeen times its actual size compared to lands near the Equator.

Since John Melish published his world map in 1818, mapmakers have come up with many different kinds of projections, but the Mercator projection is still popular. The map of Venus on page 30, made with the latest space technology, uses the projection created by Gerardus Mercator more than four hundred years ago.

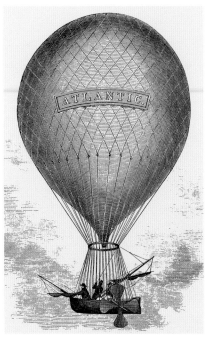

When human beings first rose above the surface of the earth, they saw the planet in a way that no mapmaker of the past ever had. From balloons in the 1700s and 1800s, then from airplanes in the 1900s, they could study the outlines of rivers and mountain ranges, of coastlines and continents. Beginning in the 1850s, cameras were used to record images from high above the earth, and aerial photography became a powerful new tool in making maps.

When satellites were first sent into orbit in the late 1950s, mapmaking took another great leap forward. Now new kinds of eyes could be used to study the earth. The image on the opposite page was cre-ated by one of these "eyes in the skies," a Landsat satellite. Produced in 1985, it shows the complicated geography of the region around San Francisco Bay in California.

Landsat is a form of remote sensing, a method of seeing the world that has changed mapmaking dramatically. Remote sensing uses scientific instruments that can observe and record the features of the earth from

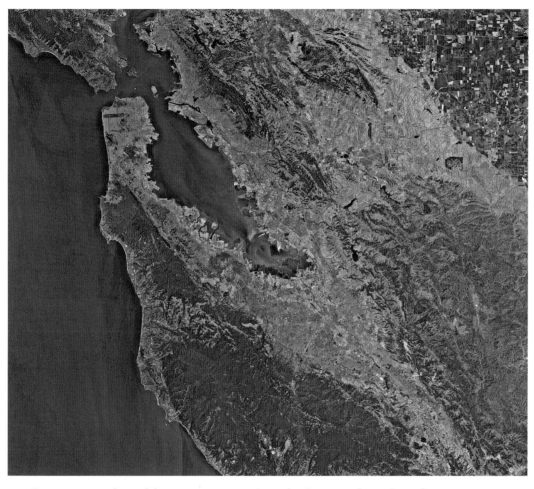

the distant vantage point of space.

The instruments carried on the Landsat satellites sense light reflected from the earth—not just the light visible to human eyes but also infrared wavelengths of light that people cannot see. This information is sent back from space in the form of radio signals and processed by computers to create detailed pictures of the earth. Landsat images can show not only physical features such as rivers and coastlines but also the kind of soil found in an area and the plants that grow there.

Images produced by remote sensing devices such as Landsat are not maps like the ones conceived and drawn by Mercator, Ortelius, and the other great mapmakers of the past. But the information they contain can be used to create all kinds of maps. Just as in the past, human eyes and minds are needed for this kind of mapmaking. People interpret the information gathered by remote sensing equipment. They operate the computers that transform this information into pictures of the world as seen through the eyes of modern science.

SECRETS OF THE OCEAN FLOOR

What lies under the waters of the world's oceans? Around 70 percent of the earth's surface is covered by water, yet until recently we knew more about the surface of the moon than about the watery parts of our own planet. All that changed in the 1990s when maps revealed some of the secrets of this hidden world.

This map of the Indian Ocean floor was created in 1997 by two American scientists, Walter Smith of the National Oceanic and Atmospheric Administration and David Sandwell of the Scripps Institution of Oceanography. They developed it from information collected by satellites orbiting the earth and ships crisscrossing the seas.

The satellites provided indirect information about the ocean floor through readings based on gravity. A Geosat satellite sent up by the U.S. Navy in the 1980s had measured the ocean's surface by bouncing microwaves off it. The measurements revealed lumps and bulges caused by the pull of gravity from ridges and other underwater features. By studying these surface variations, the scientists could get a good idea of what was on the ocean floor.

To gain more information for their maps, Smith and Sandwell used measurements of ocean depths collected by ships. These measurements were made by bouncing sound waves off the bottom and seeing how long it took for them to return. Combining ship soundings with the satellite information, the scientists were able to create a detailed picture of the ocean floor.

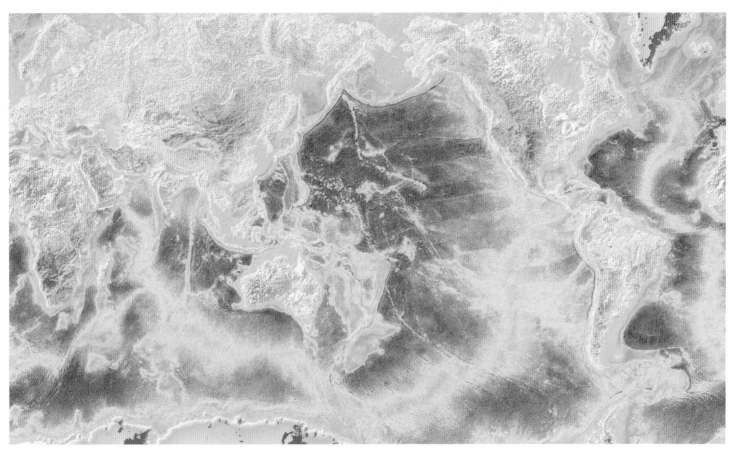

Their map uncovers many fascinating aspects of this underwater world. It shows the location of ridges and volcanoes (colored green) and indicates regions of great depth (in purple). By studying such ocean features, scientists can learn more about the tectonic plates that make up the surface of the earth and the forces causing them to move and change. The map may also provide more practical information—for example, the location of new areas for commercial fishing.

Beautiful as well as useful, this map of the ocean floor represents one of the many ways that modern science and cartography work together to expand our knowledge of the world.

MAPPING OTHER WORLDS

Mapmakers today are creating pictures not only of hidden places on the earth but also of other planets. In the 1980s, the United States and the Soviet Union sent up probes that went into orbit around Venus, the cloud-covered planet closest to the earth. Instruments on the probes bounced radar waves off the surface, revealing Venus's hidden features.

This map, made in 1982, shows some of these features. The yellow areas represent continent-like uplands that contain giant volcanoes, some taller than Mount Everest. Surrounding these regions are rolling plains of dried lava, shown in blue. Large craters produced by the impact of meteorites are scattered over the planet's surface.

Ancient astronomers named Venus for the Roman goddess of love, and modern

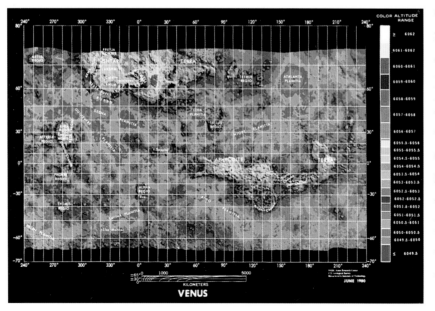

scientists have used other female names for many of the planet's features. Ishtar Terra (upper left) honors a goddess of ancient Babylonia. A crater on Ishtar is named for Sacajawea, the Indian woman who accompanied Lewis and Clark on their expedition through western North America in the 1800s.

Mapmakers in earlier times needed special skills and knowledge, but today, with the help of computers, almost anyone can create a map. A geography information system (GIS) provides the tools and information needed to produce all kinds of maps.

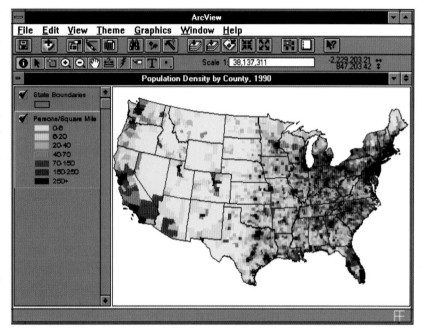

A GIS works with computer software that includes information about the physical features of the earth, about nations, states, and cities, about population and climate, and many other topics. Using a desktop computer, a mapmaker can select from this store of information to create a specific map. For example, the map on this page, made with a GIS, pictures the population density of the United States based on census figures from 1990.

When you sit down at a computer keyboard and use a GIS to create one special map, you become part of an important enterprise. You are following in the footsteps of Ptolemy, Mercator, Ortelius, and all those mapmakers of the past who did their best to represent in pictures the world and all its parts.

BOOKS ABOUT MAPS

Note: The starred books (*) will be of particular interest to young readers.

Berthon, Simon, and Andrew Robinson. *The Shape of the World: The Mapping and Discovery of the Earth.* Chicago: Rand McNally, 1991.

Brown, Lloyd A. *The Story of Maps.* New York: Dover Publications, 1979.

*Chapman, Gillian, and Pam Robso. *Maps and Mazes.* Brookfield, CT: Millbrook Press, 1993.

Crone, Gerald Roe. *Maps and Their Makers: An Introduction to the History of Cartography.* London: Hutchinson, 1968.

Goss, John. *The Mapmaker's Art.* Chicago: Rand McNally, 1993.

Hall, Stephen A. *Mapping the Next Millennium: The Discovery of New Geographies.* New York: Random House, 1992.

*Haslam, Andrew. *Maps.* Chicago: World Book, Two-Can, 1996.

*Lambert, David. *Maps and Globes.* New York: Bookwright, 1987.

*La Pierre, Yvette. *Mapping a Changing World.* New York: Thomasson-Grant & Lickle, 1996.

Makower, Joel, editor. *The Map Catalog.* New York: Vintage Books, 1992.

*Mango, Karin N. *Map-Making.* New York: J. Messner, 1984.

Schwartz, Seymour I. *Mapping of North America.* New York: H. N. Abrams, 1980.

*Smoothey, Marion. *Maps and Scale Drawings.* New York: Marshall Cavendish, 1995.

*Stefoff, Rebecca. *The Young Oxford Companion to Maps and Mapmaking.* New York: Oxford University Press, 1995.

*Taylor, Barbara. *Be Your Own Map Expert.* New York: Sterling Publishing Company, 1994.

Tooley, Ronald V. *Maps and Map-makers.* New York: Crown, 1978.

Thrower, Norman J. *Maps & Civilization: Cartography in Culture and Society.* Chicago: University of Chicago Press, 1996.

*Weiss, Harvey. *Maps: Getting from Here to There.* New York: Houghton Mifflin, 1991.

Wilford, John Noble. *The Mapmakers.* New York: Knopf, 1981.

Whitefield, Peter. *The Image of the World: 20 Centuries of World Maps.* San Francisco: Pomegranate Artbooks, 1994.

CREDITS   Illustrations courtesy of: pp. 1, 2, 7, 21, 23, 25, Library of Congress Geography and Map Division; pp. 4, 30, National Aeronautics and Space Administration; p. 5, © British Museum; pp. 9 (Add.28681 f. 9), 11 (Roy.14 C.VII f.2), British Library; pp. 13, 16, 17, 19, James Ford Bell Library, University of Minnesota; p. 12, 15, Museo Naval, Madrid; p. 27, U.S. Geological Survey, EROS Data Center; p. 29, Dr. Walter H. F. Smith, National Oceanic and Atmospheric Administration; p. 31, Environmental Systems Research Institute Inc.

Jacket front: Upper left, upper right, and lower left, Library of Congress; lower right, Dr. Walter H. F. Smith.

Back: Upper right, lower left, and symbol, James Ford Bell Library, University of Minnesota; lower right, NASA; upper left, U.S. Geological Survey, EROS Data Center.